From:

Adoption
Is Another Word for Love

Edited by Nancy McGuire Roche

 PETER PAUPER PRESS, INC.

WHITE PLAINS, NEW YORK

For my mother, Mary,
and for Anjelika

Photo credits appear on page 81.
Photos are not necessarily of
adoptive parents or children.

Designed by Heather Zschock

Text copyright © 2000
Peter Pauper Press, Inc.
202 Mamaroneck Avenue
White Plains, NY 10601
All rights reserved
ISBN 0-88088-329-4
Printed in China
7 6 5 4 3 2 1

Visit us at www.peterpauper.com

Adoption
Is Another Word
for Love

Introduction

One brilliant sunny morning, my husband and I sped through a strange, foreign city on our way to see our daughter for the first time. We had traveled for days, stayed up all night, and flown on the oldest airplane I had ever seen. We were in a country that I had feared as an enemy all through my childhood. And now, my family would be created there. I would grow to love Russia in the depths of my heart, for in my child's face is contained the great mystery and poetry of this proud country.

Our journey into family is ongoing. I thought the day we first saw our daughter would be the most special I would ever experience, but I was wrong. Our longing for this child predated even her birth. And our love for her grows ever stronger, like a tree that flowers most beautifully after careful tending.

Adoption is fulfillment. It is the end of endless waiting. It is the joy of hope actualized, created by longing, patience and grace. Adoption is an act that makes the world smaller, that leads to empathy and understanding between separate cultures and among races. It transcends physical boundaries.

Those touched by adoption, both parents and children, share membership in a special group. The words that follow tell our stories and give a glimpse into our heart of hearts.

N. McG. R.

Our children can learn that... the concept of "family" does not rest solely on biology. They can learn that love transcends many artificial boundaries frequently put into place by humans. They can learn that closing one door can open another door and another and another...

CAROLINE HARDING
adoptive parent

Adoption feels like genetic connection because it links you directly not only to your own gene pool but to the genes of all humanity, all the way to the roots from which we all originated....

[A]doption carries the added dimension of connection not only to your own tribe but beyond, widening the scope of what constitutes love, ties and family. It is a larger embrace.

ISABELLA ROSSELLINI
adoptive parent

The memories of childhood are like candles in a darkened room. We strive to illuminate yours with our love.

NANCY McGUIRE ROCHE
adoptive parent

I'm thinking about all the things I wish I had said… to people considering adoption. Like how deeply our two children have touched and enriched my life, far beyond anything that the classes and talks with social workers could have prepared me for.

JULIA LAMB
adoptive parent

To give them what I never had heals me. Some days I look at them and almost start to cry. I think, How can I love them more than I did the day before? But it keeps growing.

ROSIE O'DONNELL
adoptive parent

How can blood be thick-
er than water when the
people who gave me
water for my thirst were
not my blood relatives?

KIMBERLEA AMELING
adopted child

By choice, we have
become a family, first in
our hearts, and finally
in breath and being.
Great expectations
are good; great
experiences are better.

RICHARD FISCHER
adoptive parent

[T]ime and experience have taught me a priceless lesson: Any child you take for your own becomes your own if you give of yourself to that child. I have borne two children and had seven others by adoption, and they are all my children, equally beloved and precious.

DALE EVANS

adoptive parent

"Give up," I was told. But how could I? I wasn't thinking of him as a boy who needed adoption. In my heart he was already my son. I simply had to bring him home.

CHERYL CARTER SHOTTS
adoptive parent, adoption agency director

I did not make you
in my own image;
I created you from
the imagery of
my heart.

NANCY McGUIRE ROCHE
adoptive parent

A mother is likened unto a mountain spring that nourishes the tree at its root, but one who mothers another's child is likened unto a water that rises into a cloud and goes a long distance to nourish a lone tree in the desert.

TALMUD

Six years ago, I was living at Howrah Station (in Calcutta) without a family, and this year I got to shake the hand of the President. That's pretty special. I told him that I watched the news about how his wife visited orphanages on her trip to India, and when I got to the word "India," I started crying... I was so sad about all the kids who don't have a family...

MARJEENA GRIFFIN
adopted child

It is a colorful litany
that winds toward me
from the horizon like
a road across a rocky
desert.... And the road
ends in my arms at my
own oasis—our son.

ELIZABETH BENKO
(pseudonym)
adoptive parent

While food sustains life,
human contact sustains hope....
Somewhere along her journey
she was given hope. Gaby's
hope. The hope of a child....
It may have been the beating
of her heart pressed against
another. The human equation
that binds us all together,
where east and west do meet.

TIM WIBKING
adoptive parent

We were not separated at your birth. It was the moment at which we began our journey toward each other.

NANCY McGUIRE ROCHE
adoptive parent

That little face that had
become so familiar to me
after hours of looking at
her photo was staring
intently back at us as if to
say, "Oh here you are."
Her nanny handed her to
us and we all cried . . .

MICHELLE PALMER

adoptive parent

Charlie Henry (Jackson) adopted me and gave me his name, his love, his encouragement, discipline and a high sense of self respect.

JESSE JACKSON
adopted child

However motherhood

comes to you,

it's a miracle.

VALERIE HARPER
adoptive parent

Do you want to do something beautiful for God? There is a person who needs you. This is your chance.

MOTHER TERESA

To adopt a child is to take that
child out of poverty and loneliness
and introduce him or her to a
world of love, hope and possibility.
There is no greater achievement.

RUDOLPH W. GIULIANI

I was the 167th child to be adopted from Korea. More than 60,000 Korean children in the last forty years have made the same journey. That trip across the ocean is much more than a journey of several thousand miles. For those of us who have been adopted, it is the birth into our family.

SUSAN SOON-KEUM COX
adopted child

Mom said that what really cinched the deal was my smile. Once she saw that, she didn't want to look at any other babies.

GREG LOUGANIS
adopted child

The work of parenting is the ultimate task for which all our learn-ing is preparation.

NANCY McGUIRE ROCHE
adoptive parent

My wish is that children
be treated as people,
and not as property;
that their rights as
human beings on the
planet, to food, shelter,
education and health,
be taken seriously.

OPRAH WINFREY

We must work tirelessly to make sure that every boy and girl in America who is up for adoption has a family waiting to reach him or her... This is a season of miracles, and perhaps there is no greater miracle than finding a loving home for a child who needs one.

BILL CLINTON
adopted child

People ask me, "What about gay adoptions? Interracial? Single Parent?" I say, "Hey fine, as long as it works for the child and the family is responsible." My big stand is this: Every child deserves a home and love. Period.

DAVE THOMAS,
founder of Wendy's
adopted child

If a child is born
and raised in a home that
is loving and nurturing,
where there is complete
truth about who we are,
you can't give a child
any greater place from
which to fly.

AMANDA BEARSE
adoptive parent

Though she wasn't a blood relative, people say we looked alike. She was short, only five feet and one-quarter inch tall...and had a high forehead, just like me. Yet my clearest and fondest memory of my mother is her laughter...

SCOTT HAMILTON
adopted child

We look at adoption as a very sacred exchange. It was not done lightly on either side. I would dedicate my life to this child.

JAMIE LEE CURTIS
adoptive mother

Both the courage and trust of those who decide to place their babies for adoption and the enthusiasm of those who adopt them are overwhelmingly vindicated by the tens of thousands of successful adoptions that take place in this country every year.

THE NEW YORKER

editorial

[G]rowing up in a nest of foster children plunged me at an extremely early age into some of the more tragic situations that confront helpless people. And that awareness which never leaves a person and colors all that he or she does in later life can be of enormous value... It influenced all I would write.

JAMES A. MICHENER
adopted child

There is no doubt in my mind that being adopted affects parenting in a profound way. But how it manifests itself is as idiosyncratic as each parent, as unique as each child.... We can only do our best to follow our hearts, to watch both ourselves and our children with a compassionate eye, and to find our own place on the ever-tilting balance beam of parenthood.

SUSAN ITO
adopted child

I was thirty-five years old.
I hadn't given up hope
that I would meet the
man of my dreams, but
I was open to the fact that
I might not..., and that's
okay, but in the meantime,
I want to have a family.

MICHELLE PFEIFFER
adoptive parent

As an adopted child, I was constantly trying to find out who I was.... I tried everything because I wanted to challenge myself. I played music, played sports, tried to be a politician.

That's my advice: Try anything! If you never give up you'll be successful.

DAN O'BRIEN
adopted child

I realized at the start that whether a child is biological or adopted, one does not know all the ingredients in the package. That is what growth is all about. A child is the slowest flower in the world, opening petal by petal, revealing the developing personality within.

ROBERT KLOSE

adoptive parent

Somehow my last image of the orphanage strikes me as the most poignant. The children are sleeping peacefully in the nearby bedroom. I remember imagining them dreaming of some day having a real family and a new life.... A sudden shaft of sunlight shines brightly across the chairs and fills the room with hope.

DARCY KIEFEL
adoptive parent

He who can reach
a child's heart
can reach the
world's heart.

RUDYARD KIPLING

Somehow destiny
comes into play.
These children end
up with you and you
end up with them.
It's something
quite magical.

NICOLE KIDMAN
adoptive parent

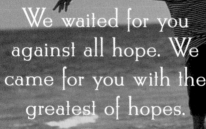

We waited for you against all hope. We came for you with the greatest of hopes.

NANCY McGUIRE ROCHE
adoptive parent

I sometimes told the other
orphans I had real wonderful
parents who were away on
a long trip and would come
for me any time, and once
I wrote a postcard to myself
and signed it from Mother and
Daddy... I wanted to think
it was true. And maybe if
I thought it was true it
would come true.

MARILYN MONROE
adopted child

I learned that my only defense to be not consumed by these stereotypes is to know who I am. These experiences demanded me to know that I am an American. I am a Korean and I am an adoptee, and most importantly I am my own person.

ASHLEY YONG-SOO LEWIS
adopted child

Moses, Oedipus, King Arthur, the Ugly Duckling, Superman, and Luke Skywalker all have some things in common. They were all adopted and they are some of our culture's major self-realization archetypes. Without the search, there would have been no story.

ABIGAIL LOVETT
adopted child

But as I grew older—and I feel even more strongly about it today—I realized that every adopted child should be told the truth at the earliest possible moment.... The truth is that you chose this child because you wanted him and that proves your love.

ART LINKLETTER
adopted child

Quinton will always know he's adopted. We'll tell him as soon as he can possibly understand. When he's 18 the record can be opened and, if he wishes, he will be able to seek out his birth parents.... It doesn't bother me at all. I don't think the capacity to love is limited to just one mother and dad.

LONI ANDERSON
adoptive parent

He [has] probably never
been in an orphanage and
seen little kids without moms
and dads. And I had been in
a lot of them. I've seen the
other side, the sick side of
'em and the lonely side.
And I tried to take up the
space. We've had 4 adopted
and 1 foster child. It's been
a wonderful family life.

ROY ROGERS
adoptive parent

It has been said that adoption is more like a marriage than a birth: two (or more) individuals, each with their own unique mix of needs, patterns, and genetic history, coming together with love, hope, and commitment for a joint future. You become a family not because you share the same genes, but because you share love for each other.

JOAN McNAMARA

adoptive parent

Dear Lord, I do not ask
that Thou shouldst give
me some high work of thine,
some noble calling or
some wondrous task.
Give me a little hand
to hold in mine.

ANONYMOUS

Now I have the
time and money to
enjoy my little girl,
and I intend to spend
as much time as
I can with her…
she's a gem.

ED McMAHON
adoptive parent

And now it makes every day like Christmas. I can't wait to see him in the morning, I can't wait for him to wake up.

KIRSTIE ALLEY
adoptive parent

I must remember
to encourage others
to do this marvelous
thing—adopting
a hyperactive,
sweating lunatic
unable to change
her own diaper.

TAMA JANOWITZ
adoptive parent

A fundamental character of all humans is that we are flawed; there is no perfect person, we simply just live and survive and hopefully help as many people as we can along the way do just that. It amazes me how resilient we humans are. With a little guidance and support we can conquer anything, no matter how big the monster.

ROXANNE AGUR
adopted child

Many of the parents I interviewed... reason that the extraordinary circumstances which led them to that particular child at that particular time in that particular place were simply miraculous and therefore unique in human experience.

CAROLE S. TURNER
adoptive parent

Having been adopted, I really have a strong sense—a necessity almost—for stability. A foundation where my family is concerned. [Success] would be meaningless without anyone to share it with.

FAITH HILL
adopted child

And then it seemed like we had never been without her, like we had always known her face, her spirit. Now I can't imagine living without her. What if we had given birth and had never gone to China?

Where would Sallie Bai be now, and how would we live without her? We thank God that didn't happen.

ELIZABETH GILLESPIE
adoptive parent

As if our hands, our sides,
voices, and minds
Had been incorporate.
So we grew together,
Like to a double cherry,
seeming parted,
But yet an union in partition.

WILLIAM SHAKESPEARE,
A Midsummer Night's Dream

We got married in our 20's and had two children very young. Spiritually and intellectually, we're better equipped now. And... we weren't ready to stop being parents.

ROBERT URICH
adoptive parent

One gets only a day
or two in an entire
lifetime as incredible
as the day we first
saw your face.

NANCY McGUIRE ROCHE
adoptive parent

Adoptive parents are special and there is a bond that binds us, but has no name. We understand without words the precious gifts that we have been entrusted with.

MARTHA OSBORNE
adoptive parent

In short, they are family.
They are bright, loving
children and it seems as
though they have always
been here.... We claim
these two children—and
they have claimed us.

MARYBETH LAMBE
adoptive parent

Let go of your
ambitions. Come
let's change
the world.

ST. FRANCIS XAVIER

Photo Credits